Nashville Freedom Schools 2018

"**Freedom School is a good place to be.**"
– Alexander, a Nashville Freedom School scholar

Ideas into Books: Westview®
Kingston Springs, Tennessee

Ideas into Books®
W E S T V I E W
P.O. Box 605
Kingston Springs, TN 37082
www.ideasintobooks.net
www.publishedbywestview.com

Copyright © 2018 Nashville Freedom School Partnership©

All rights reserved, including the right to reproduction, storage, transmittal, or retrieval, in whole or in part in any form.

The Nashville Freedom School Partnership logo, created by Chicago graphic artist, Ted Glascoe, celebrates the pursuit of learning inherent in all young people.

ISBN 978-1-62880-156-9

First edition, July 2018

We Are Nashville Freedom Schools!

Nashville Freedom Schools© are a local expression of the national Children's Defense Fund Freedom Schools©, a six-week summer program created in 1995 years ago by the D.C.-based advocacy group led by Marian Wright Edelman.

Ms. Edelman, a veteran of the 1960s Civil Rights Movement, has built CDF to ensure a level playing field for all children. The Children's Defense Fund champions policies and programs that lift children out of poverty, protect them from abuse and neglect, and lobby for their access to health care, quality education and a moral and spiritual foundation.

The CDF Freedom Schools® program seeks to build strong, literate, and empowered children prepared to make a difference in themselves, their families, communities, nation and world today. By providing summer and after-school reading enrichment for children and teens who might otherwise not have access to books, the CDF Freedom Schools© program plays a much needed role in helping to curb summer learning loss and close achievement gaps. This work is a vital step in breaking the "cradle-to-prison pipeline," which entraps children of color living in poverty.

In partnership with local congregations, schools, colleges and universities, community organizations, and secure juvenile justice facilities the CDF Freedom Schools© program boosts student motivation to read, generates more positive attitudes toward learning, increases self-esteem and connects the needs of children and families to the resources of their communities.

Since 1995, more than 137,000 pre K-12 children in more than 110 U.S. cities have had a CDF Freedom Schools© experience and more than 16,000 college students and young adult staff have been trained by CDF to deliver this empowering model.

Freedom Schools© focus on expanding children's minds and experiences, so that they want to learn, understand their value to their communities, and gain skills to help them succeed in school and life. The theme each summer is "I Can Make A Difference," and the assigned books and activities—from field trips to art classes—reinforce the idea that young people are a force to change their homes, schools, communities, and nation for the better.

The Nashville Freedom School Partnership© was registered in 2014 as nonprofit agency, with the goal of creating summertime enrichment programs using CDF Freedom Schools©' curriculum and pedagogy. These program target Nashville's children who most need them. Since then, more than 400 children in grades K-8 have participated.

Our programs are offered at no charge to participating families, the majority of whom live near or below the state poverty line. We raise money through private donors, foundations, and grants to provide all books, meals, snacks, field trips, and STEM and artistic classes and experiences for our scholars and their families.

Our partners organization who host, fund, and support Freedom Schools in Nashville included local churches, synagogues, nonprofit agencies, performance groups and artists, schools and colleges, and local businesses.

Our local Children's Defense Fund Team members (led by Dr. Janet Wolf of the national CDF staff) have been invaluable in spreading the word and recruiting parents, scholars, interns, volunteers and donors for Nashville Freedom Schools.

Ashiya Swan, formerly a site director, is now a frequent volunteer and member of the Nashville Freedom School Partnership board of directors.

Servant Leader Interns

Nashville Freedom Schools could not operate without the energy and creativity of our Servant Leader Interns. These college-age young people (and recent college or graduate school alums) are on the front line of caring for, nurturing, and mentoring our scholars.

Chosen through a competitive screening process, these dynamic young adults must be in their sophomores year or higher, enrolled in a four-year college or graduate school to even qualify for an interview. Further, they must each have a 3.0+ grade-point average and demonstrate exceptional moral character, maturity, passion, and responsibility.

Servant Leader Interns (SLIs) undergo training by the national Children's Defense Fund team on how to teach using our Integrated Reading Curriculum© to classes of ten students each over the six-week summer course.

In early June, 2018 Servant Leader Interns Kim Morris, Kaylah Lockett, Chioma Tait, Tarif Hunt, and Terry Blackburn headed to Knoxville, Tenn., for national Children's Defense Fund Freedom School© training. More than 1,800 interns from around the country come together annually for training, community building, and networking at the start of each summer's classes as they prepare to teach in summer Freedom Schools© around the country.

Since we began in 2014, the Servant Leader Interns for **Nashville Freedom Schools** have come from as far away as New York, Texas and Jamaica, representing prestigious colleges and universities such as Howard University, Fisk University, Vanderbilt University, Clark-Atlanta University, the New School for Social Research, University of Memphis, Middle Tennessee State University and Tennessee State University.

Several our past interns have gone on to graduate and get jobs (including several who became teachers and social workers, in part because of their Freedom School© experience), and still they come back in the summer to work at Nashville Freedom Schools. Still other are promoted to administrative leadership in Freedom Schools© because of their passion and talents.

2018 Servant Leader Interns Tarif Hunt, Tiara Morton, and Angel Frazier in a team-building exercise.

EmmaJulia Jones, a graduate of Centre College and now a public school teacher in Nashville, has been a Servant Leader Intern with us since 2016. She says her experience with Freedom Schools©, "made me more aware of the inequities that our scholars may face and highlighted the importance of literacy for all children. It confirmed for me that teaching is what I am meant to do."

Chris Johnson, an alumnus of Clark-Atlanta University, who joined Nashville Freedom Schools in 2015, agrees. "Being a mentor to the kids means that I am helping us build a better future. One of these scholars may end up giving me a job," laughs Chris, who is currently applying for law school.

"I want them to remember that part of being a great leader is giving back to your community. I'm glad to give back."

The 2018 staff at Gordon Memorial Freedom School enjoy a light moment. Gordon team members were, front row, from left Chris Johnson, T.J. Debnam, and Angel Frazier and, back row, from left Tim Cunningham, Terry Blackburn, MacKenzie Milon, Ti'Ara Clark, Anah Sinkfield, and Kimberly Morris.

The 2018 Watson Grove Freedom Schools staff dressed up one week to model professionalism for their scholars. Front row, from left: EmmaJulia Jones, Cynthia Anderson, Tiara Morton, Kaylah Lockett, and Lance Richards. Second row, from left: Luther Young, Tarif Hunt, Ben Johnson, Lyante Savala, and Chioma Tait.

Our 2018 Nashville Freedom School staff members

(*denotes staff member who has served two years or more)

Coordinators Cynthia Anderson of Watson Grove and T.J. Debnam, from Gordon Memorial.

Gordon Servant Leader Interns

Terry Blackburn
Ti'Ara Clark
Timothy Cunningham*
Angel Frazier
Chris Johnson*
Kimberly Morris
Anah Sinkfield

Watson Grove Servant Leader Interns

Tarif Hunt
Benjamin Johnson
EmmaJulia Jones
Kaylah Lockett
Tiara Morton
Lance Richards
Chioma Tate
Lyante Savala*

Gordon Memorial United Methodist Church Freedom School

MacKenzie Milon, former SLI, Project Director
Tijuan "T.J." Debnamn, former SLI, Site Coordinator

T.J. Debnam (left), 2018 graduate of Vanderbilt Divinity School and young people's pastor at Gordon Memorial United Methodist Church, and MacKenzie Milon, who this spring earned a master's degree from the school of social work at Howard University, lead the 2018 Freedom School at Gordon Memorial Church. Both started as Servant Leader Interns and were promoted because of their passion, and their excellent mentoring and administrative skills.

Gordon Servant Leader Interns

Terry Blackburn

2018 Servant Leader Intern Terry Blackburn leads Gordon Memorial scholars in a morning cheer.

Ti'Ara Clark

New in 2018, Servant Leader Intern Ti'Ara Clark of Fisk University, was especially good at encouraging scholars to express themselves during discussions.

Timothy Cunningham

Veteran Servant Leader Intern Tim Cunningham is a founding member of the Nashville Freedom School staff. A graduate of Middle Tennessee State University, he reads with scholars Donovan and Paige (above), then works with scholars on a group project (right).

Angel Frazier

A student at Fisk University, Angel Frazier was a new Servant Leader Intern at the 2018 Freedom School at Gordon Memorial United Methodist Church.

Chris Johnson

Chris Johnson, a graduate of Clark-Atlanta
who has been with Freedom Schools© since 2015, leads the morning *Harambee*
(taken from the Kiswahili word for, "let's pull together") at Gordon Memorial.
Harambee is a time for music, dance, cheers, and centering at the start of the Freedom School© day.

Kimberly Morris

Kimberly Morris, a native of Jamaica and a student at Fisk University, is a 2018 Servant Leader Intern at the Gordon Memorial Freedom School.

Anah Sinkfield

New to the Nashville Freedom Schools' staff this year, Anah chose a camping theme for her classroom.

Former scholar and junior intern Sierra, left, and scholars Tamia, Isaiah, and Aniyah, meet Clara Ester, a United Methodist deaconess from Alabama, who worked in the Civil Rights Movement with the late Dr. Martin Luther King. Ms. Ester was one of a team of women from the national racial justice team of United Methodist Women who hosted 2018 Nashville Freedom School scholars and staff for dinner and conversation this summer.

Watson Grove Missionary Baptist Church Freedom School

**Luther Young, former SLI, Project Director (above)
Cynthia Anderson, Site Coordinator (right)**

Luther Young

Luther Young, a 2018 graduate of Vanderbilt Divinity School
and a candidate for ministry in the Christian Church (Disciples of Christ),
leads the news Nashville Freedom Schools site at Watson Grove Missionary Baptist Church.

Cynthia Anderson

Cynthia Anderson, a veteran Metro Nashville teacher, served as site coordinator of the 2018 Freedom School at Watson Grove Baptist Church.

Watson Grove Servant Leader Interns

Tarif Hunt

Fisk University student Tarif Hunt was a first-year Servant Leader Intern at the newest Nashville Freedom School site at Watson Grove Baptist Church in South Nashville.

Benjamin Johnson

Benjamin Johnson, a 2018 graduate of East Tennessee State University, is in his third year as a Servant Leader Intern at Nashville Freedom Schools.

EmmaJulia Jones

Outstanding intern EmmaJulia Jones, a favorite friend and confidante,
has been a Nashville Freedom School teacher for three summers.

Kaylah Lockett

2018 Intern Kaylah Lockett (center), a student at Western Kentucky University, chose a teamwork theme for her classroom.

Tiara Morton

Tiara Morton (above and below, in her classroom at the Watson Grove Freedom School) loves reading aloud to her scholars and encouraging them to stretch their reading abilities.

Lance Richards,

Fisk University graduate Lance Richards (left and below with scholars) has taught in Nashville Freedom Schools for three years. In 2018, he was assigned as a Servant Leader Intern at the Watson Grove site.

Chioma Tate

New 2018 intern Chioma Tait of Howard University, had a great class this year.

Lyante Savala

Lyante, an alumni of Fisk University, now a Nashville public school teacher, has been with Nashville Freedom Schools since he was an undergraduate. Lyante returned again this summer as a teaching intern for Freedom School in Nashville.

Below:
Lyante teaches the daily lesson at Watson Grove.

The West End Junior Internship at Nashville Freedom Schools

In 2010, members of West End United Methodist Church created **TIME**, a summer employment initiative for North Nashville teenagers to help them gain job skills and work experience, and connect with positive adult mentors.

In spring 2017, West End Church joined with Nashville Freedom Schools and transformed **TIME** into a **Junior Intern** program, through which North Nashville teens apply to work for a $1,000 stipend and learn valuable work and team-building skills.

West End members and the **Nashville Freedom Schools** team developed the job description and duties, asked teens and parents to sign a covenant governing attendance and commitment to the job, and matched youth with mentors. West End Church provides the funding for junior intern salaries, and Freedom School© supervisors and volunteers offer on-the-job training and life skills. The Rev. Ray and Phyllis Sells, and Ellen Wolfe, West End's volunteer coordinator, organize the mentors (and serve as mentors themselves). In 2018, Ashiya Swan, a member of the Nashville Freedom Schools board of directors, and a specialist in restorative justice, self-care, and mindfulness, led the teens in life-skill classes.

Since this West End-Freedom School partnership began, 20 fantastic and talented Junior Interns—all high school students in grades 10-12—have served at our summer sites. The teens offer their unique talents, including majorette skills, rapping and poetry, drumming and music, leadership and organization. They also meet together twice a week with their mentors and for life lessons on dating, making positive decisions and self-care.

Our 2018 Junior Interns:

Jaylen Craig
Keishon Dalton
Ta'Kensnia Dowell
Jonesha Ferguson
Marquisha Harvey
Erille Majors
Tiara McCauley
Donnell Sandifer
Jeramieon "J.T." Teasley

Thanks to our 2018 West End Church mentors: Doug Doss, John Hill, Lynn Linebaugh Jones, David McNeel, Phyllis Sells, Ray Sells, James Sewell, Kevin Warner, Ellen Wolfe, Jackie York.

Junior Interns Watson Grove

Junior Interns Gordon Memorial

Thanks to a partnership with and funding from West End United Methodist Church, Nashville Freedom Schools also offers a Junior Internship, through which older teens gain job skills, money-management, and life skills, while earning a stipend. The 2018 Junior Interns are: (top, from left, at Watson Grove): Donnell Sandifer, Marquisha Harvey, Erille Majors and Tiara McCauley; and (bottom from left, at Gordon Memorial) Jeramieon Teasley, Keishon Dalton, Jaylen Craig, Ta'Kensnia Dowell, and Jonesha Ferguson.

Freedom School friendship.

Celebrating Us!
Books That Boost Our Pride and Potential

An important aspect of Nashville Freedom Schools is our award-winning **Integrated Reading Curriculum©,** which features books by and about African-Americans, Latinos, and other people of color around the world.

Freedom Schools© believe that books can unlock the door to children's dreams and unlimited potential. The books used in the Freedom School© curriculum are carefully chosen and they represent the best work of the country's best writers and illustrators, and children across the nation deserve to have access to them.

With the help of well-prepared and caring adults, these books have the power to help children better understand themselves and the world, and to instill in them a lifelong love of reading.

There are weekly activities to help staff and scholars reflect on the following weekly themes of making a difference in Self, Family, Community, Country, World, and with Hope, Education and Action.

These uplifting stories remind our children and teens that they can and do make a difference in our world. Children's Defense Fund© Founder Marian Wright Edelman reminds us, "If you can see it, you can BE it!" Central to our work is instilling in our children and teens that THEY can and do make a difference, starting right now!

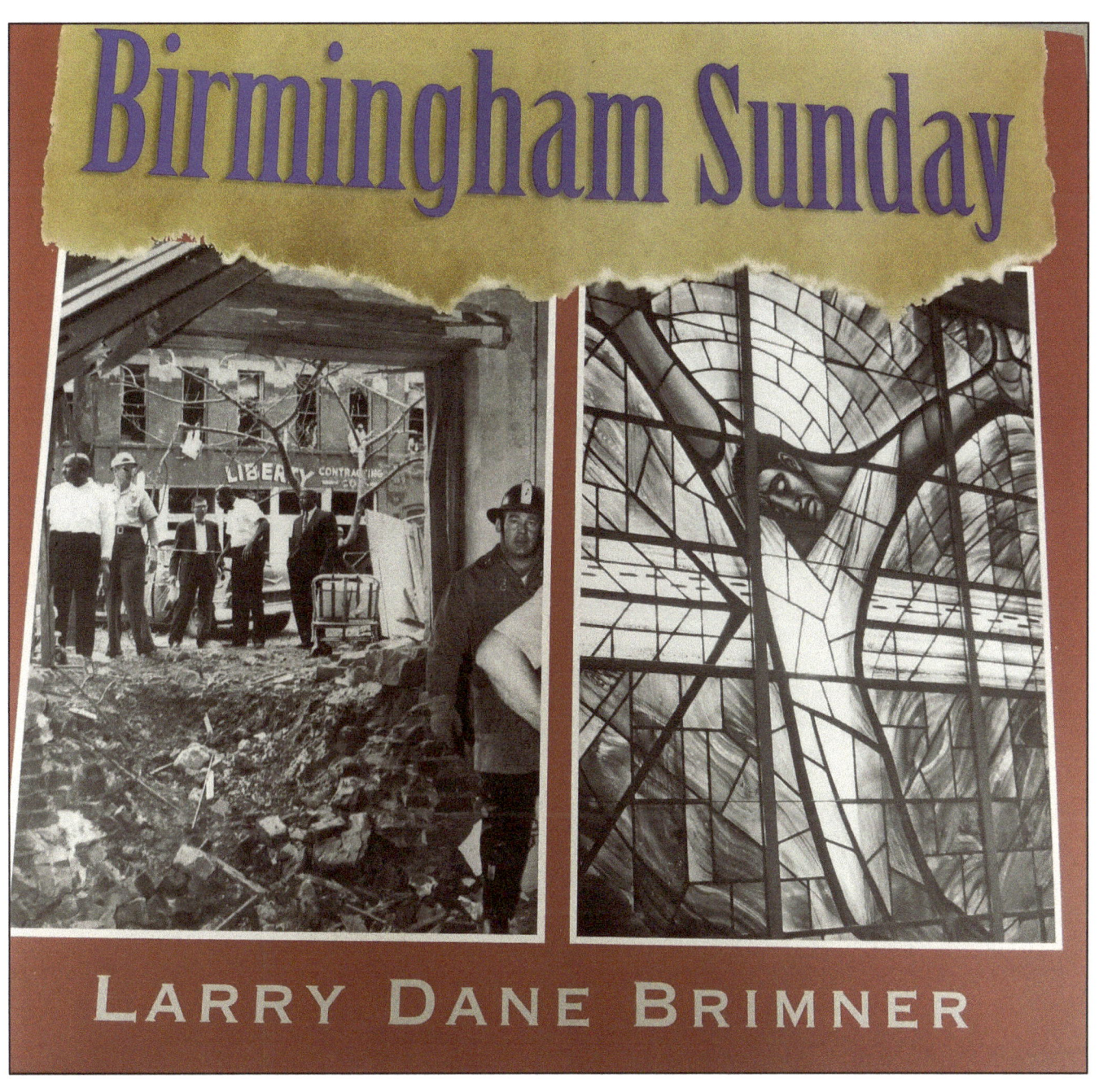

All books pictured are part of the *Integrated Reading Curriculum*© developed by the Children's Defense Fund© to boost scholars own sense of self-worth, cultural and community pride, critical thinking skills, and to encourage them to be agents for positive change.

Dear,

Little Rock Nine....

Thank you for stopping school segregation, and for sacrificing your lives just for future generations.

Thank you for not being selfish and thanks!

Sincerely, Taylor Dearin

Dear Little Rock Nine,

I would give you full marks for confidence and bravery. You changed the course of history for what you did. No one else had the confidence to do all the things you did. Thank you very much for everything!

Love,
Anyinna

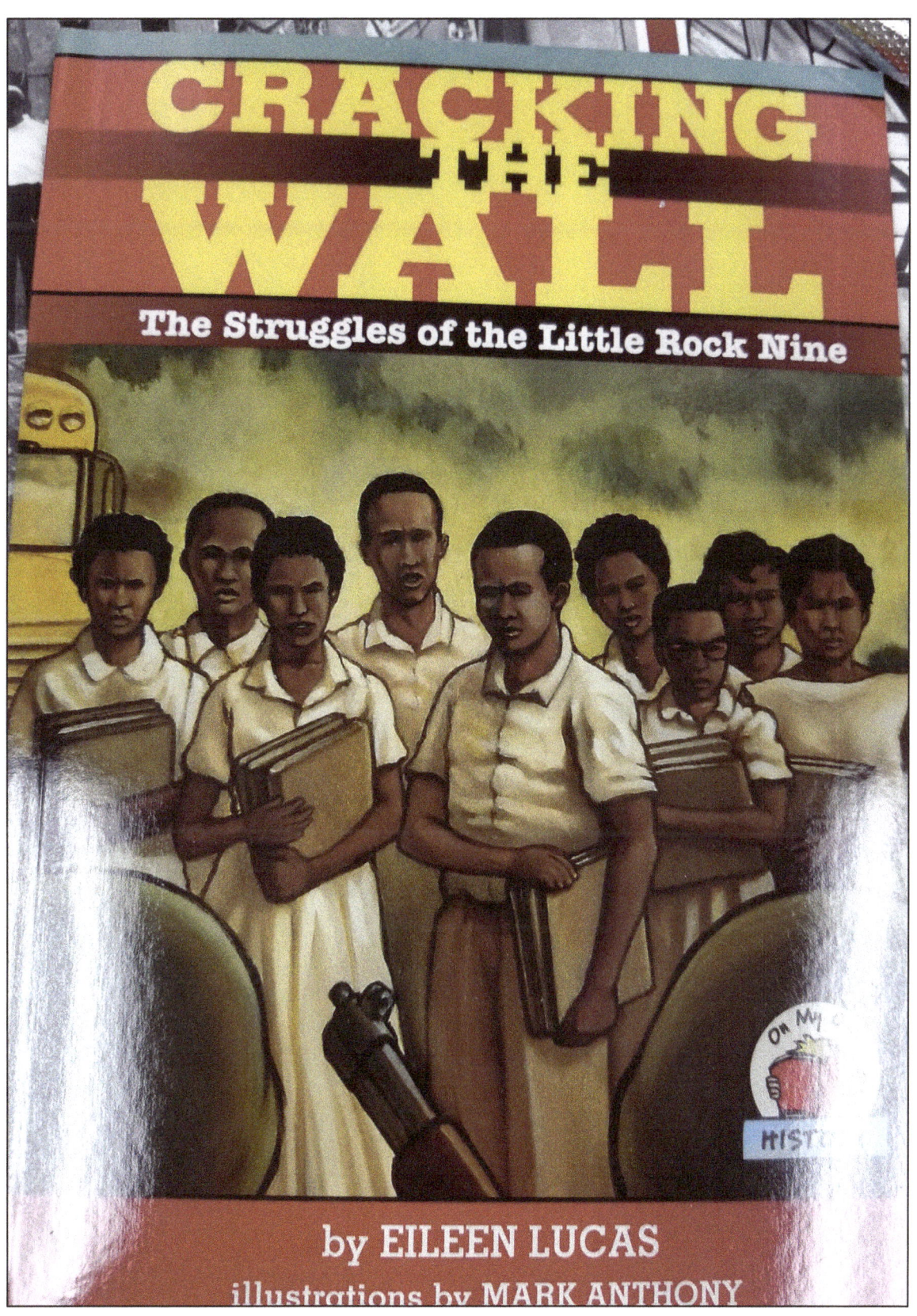

Book about unsung Civil Rights hero Claudette Colvin, who refused to give up her seat on the bus long before Rosa Parks, another hero, made headlines doing the same.

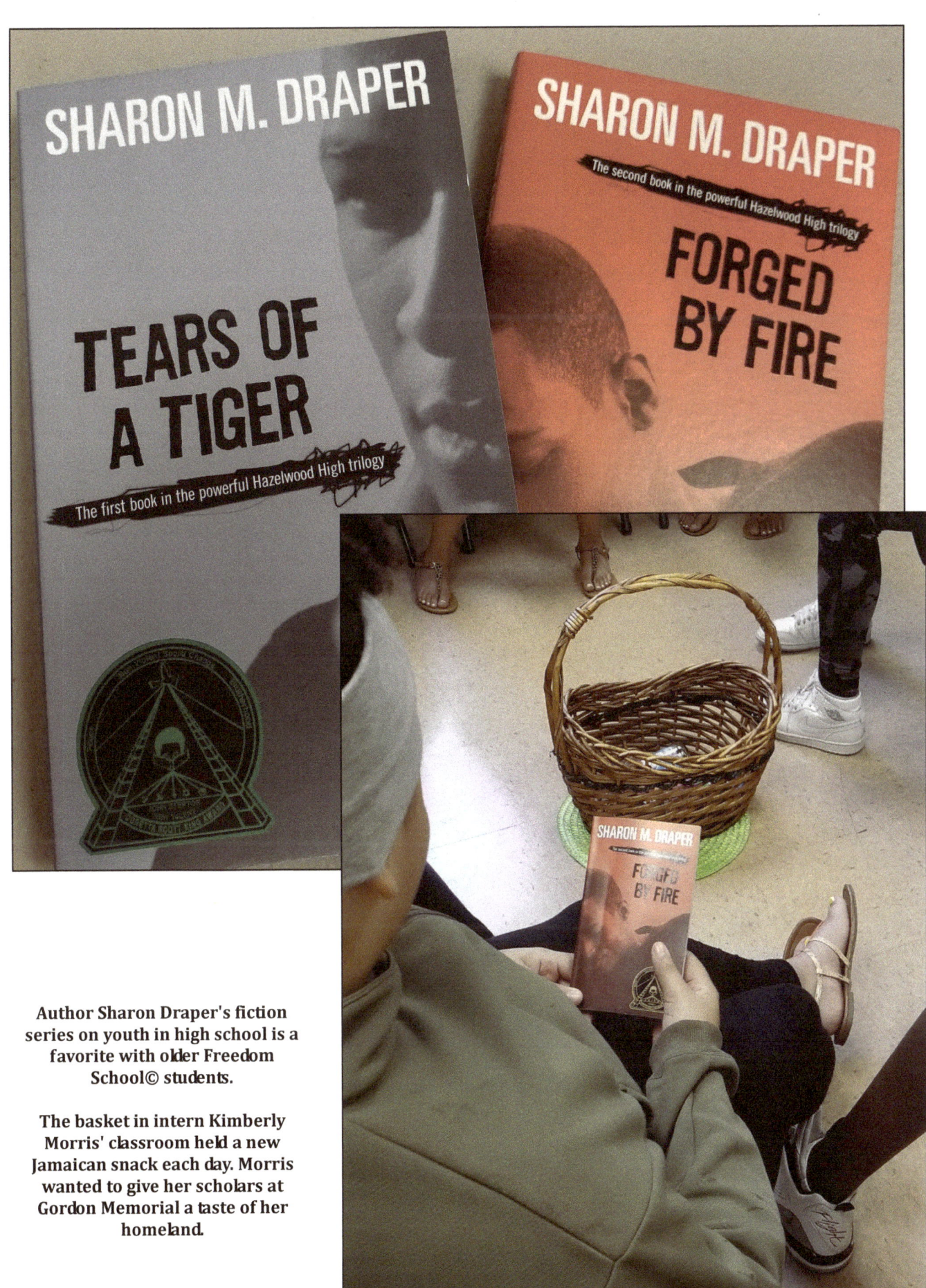

Author Sharon Draper's fiction series on youth in high school is a favorite with older Freedom School© students.

The basket in intern Kimberly Morris' classroom held a new Jamaican snack each day. Morris wanted to give her scholars at Gordon Memorial a taste of her homeland.

LET THE CHILDREN MARCH

Monica Clark-Robinson

Illustrated by Frank Morrison

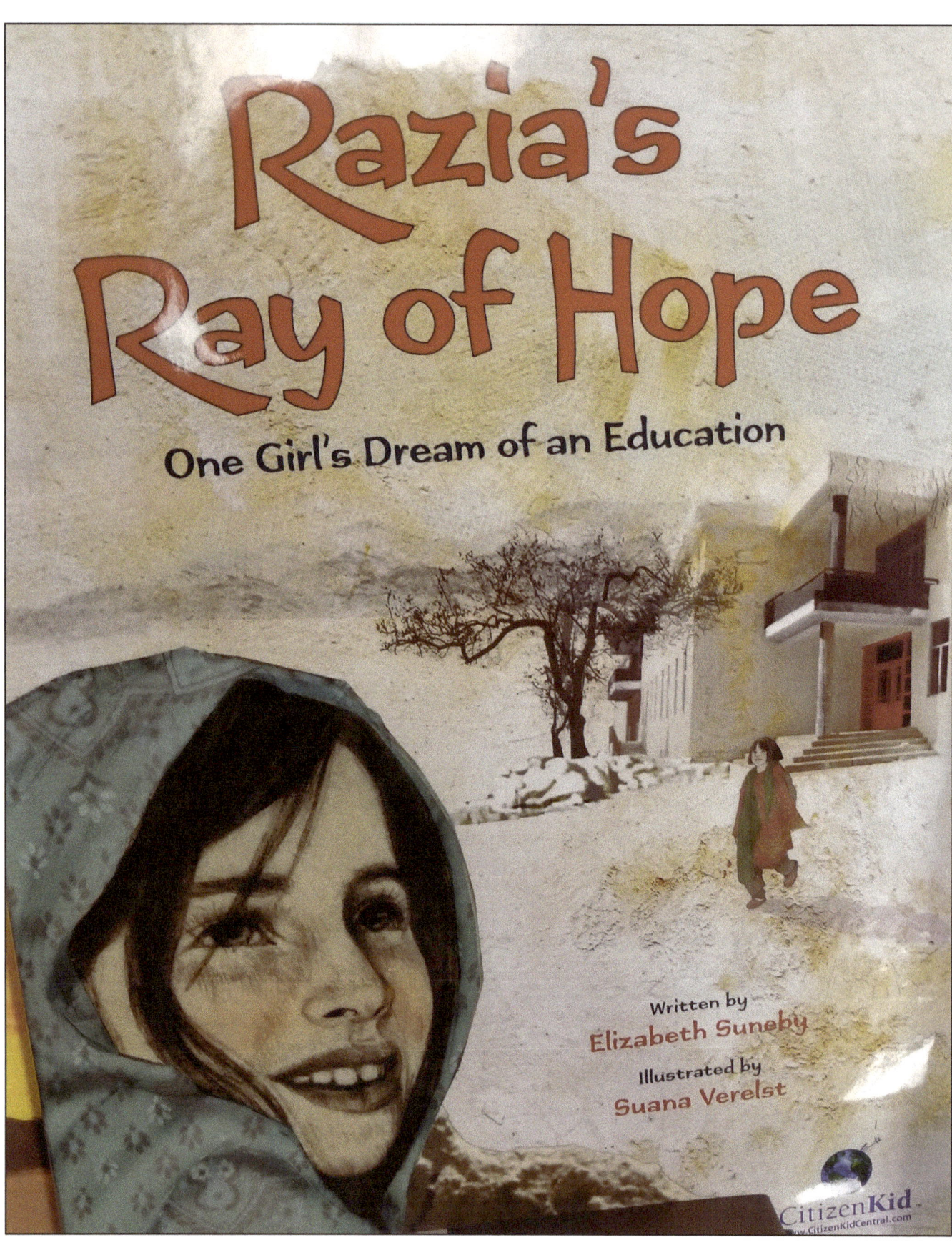

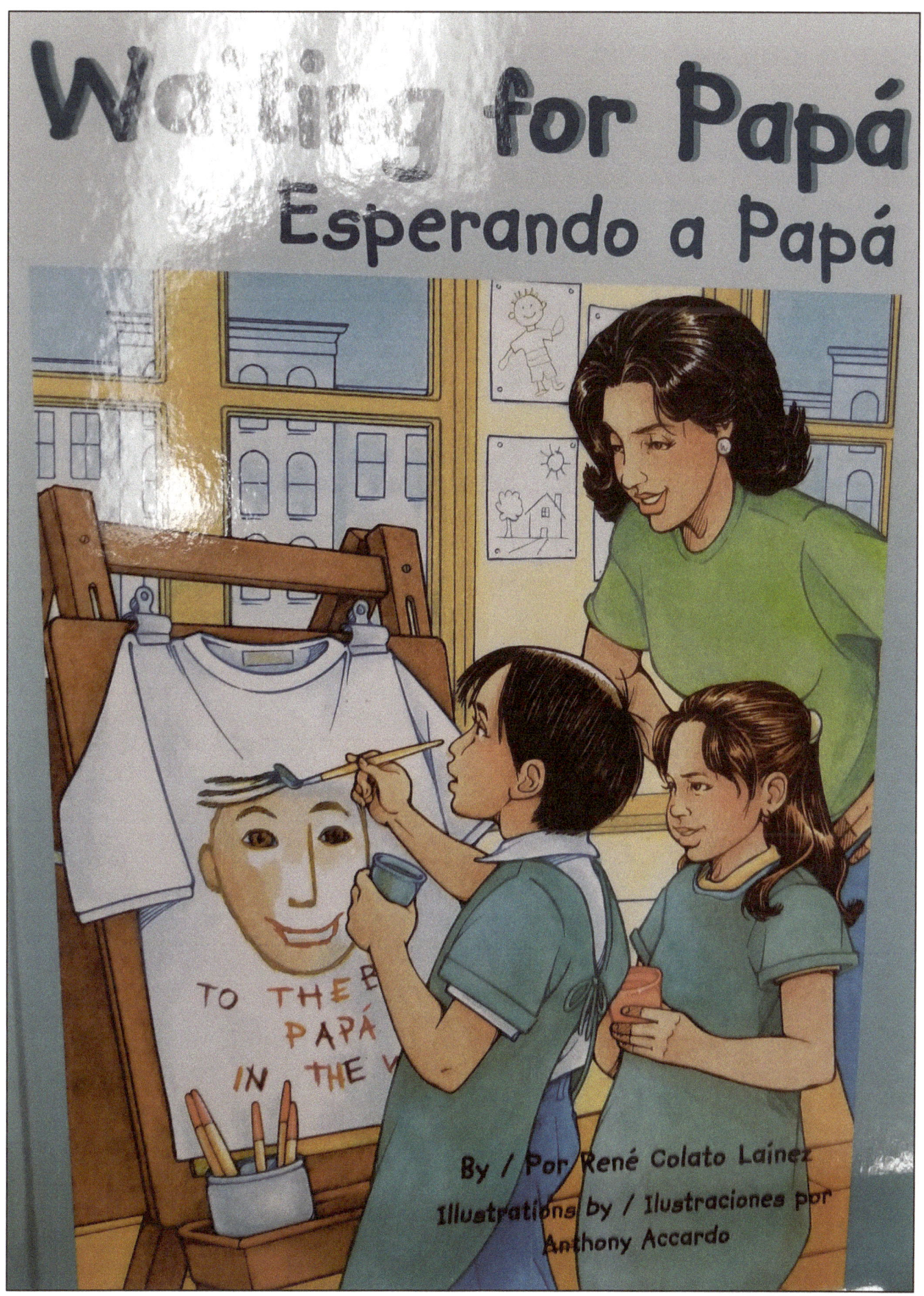

Parent Empowerment

A growing edge for Nashville Freedom Schools is our work networking, empowering, and equipping parents to better advocate for the needs of their families. A majority of our scholars are from communities where food insecurity, lack of safe and affordable housing, under-resourced public schools, and lack of public services are typical.

Many of our parents are overwhelmed and under-supported, yet they have ideas, energy, and dreams to make life better for themselves and other families.

Each week during the summer, parents of Freedom School© students come together for dinner and conversation. They share their struggles, their hopes, and their ideas for changing systems for the better to benefit themselves and the community.

In 2018, parents talked to education reform advocate Dr. Maury Nation of Vanderbilt University about the impact of harsh, "zero-tolerance" policies on their children attending Nashville public schools. They participated in question-and-answer sessions with Metro Nashville School teachers about rights of parents and scholars when a child has an IEP. They heard the story of criminal justice reform advocate Rahim Buford, who told his own story of incarceration and how he now works with Juvenile Court to keep other poor children of color from the hostility of the streets and the criminal justice system.

Parents who participate in our weekly meetings agree that sharing one another's stories, eating together, and hearing from people who care about them and their families all serve to uplift and inspire them. Further, they say they want to build a stronger network to advocate for needed changes in the public school system and other systems that directly affect their families and livelihood.

Opposite page: Education reform advocate Dr. Maury Nation of Vanderbilt University leads a discussion at the 2018 Freedom School on how Black parents can better lobby for school discipline policies that restore relationships rather that criminalize children and youth.

This page, top: Rahim Buford, a criminal justice advocate, led parent conversations about how to keep kids focused and out of the criminal justice system.

This page, bottom: Parents of the Freedom School at Watson Grove meet to encourage one another and to share more about how they advocate and support their families.

Gordon Memorial was the first congregation in Nashville to welcome the Nashville Freedom School Partnership in 2014; this site serves scholars in grade 4-8. Thanks to Pastor Charles White Jr. and other Gordon members for their unflagging support.

The Rev. John Faison Jr., lead pastor at Watson Grove Missionary Baptist Church, was the Read-Aloud guest at our opening day of the new 2018 Freedom School at his church. More than 60 children in grades K-8 attended our new South Nashville site.

Bearing Fruit: The Nashville Freedom School Difference

The scholars of Nashville Freedom Schools are among the most resilient, most inquisitive, and hope-filled children and teens in the city. What do we say that? Because they come to classes each day, against many obstacles, and play, read, learn, sing, dance, engage, smile, and think.

It is tough sometimes. Liana* showed up in tears one morning, because her mother had just been taken to jail and Liana, 9, had to call her grandmother to bring her to Freedom School. Jonathan* is a big 12-year-old who, last year, was ridiculed by other schoolmates because of his low-reading scores. They didn't know that his mother had recently died in an accident, and he was doing good just to get up and dress himself each day.

Jatasha's family slept in the car last night, because they were evicted; yet, they show up eager to see Freedom School friends and mentors. Trey* stutters. Alaysia* is hungry, because she hasn't eaten since her Freedom School lunch the day before. Gary* has a talent for drawing and painting, but his daddy—who works two jobs to support Gary and his sister—can't afford art lessons. So Gary looks forward to the volunteer art teachers who come to teach at Freedom School.

Each of these children is a scholar, a leader, a celebrated A-student at Nashville Freedom Schools. While we test scholars before and at the end of the six weeks to measure their gains in reading, we already know that their site-word fluency and critical-thinking abilities are growing. We push them to push themselves; they learn and share cultural pride and teamwork. They play new games and learn new skills.

A teen boy discovers the wonder of using a needle and thread to mend his shirt, thanks to a volunteer grandmother. A first-grader with a deaf best friend learns how to say, "What's up?" from a volunteer who is a teacher for hearing-impaired children. A fifth-grader hears a cello for the first time, as a volunteer and professional musician—who is big and dark and beautiful like him—invites his class to sing along.

<*Not their real names>

Gordon scholar Di'icis, leads the morning celebration.

Each morning, during our *Harambee* celebration (a morning time of gathering, singing, and dancing, named for a Kiswahili word meaning, "let's pull together") the scholars become a team, a tribe, and a community. Across barriers of race and culture, class and language, formally educated and the school of the streets, scholars, interns, volunteers, parents, guest tutors, artists, and teachers sing the words of the national motivational song for CDF Freedom Schools©, "There's something inside so strong/I know that I can make it."

A guest musician from Fisk University shares her talent during our morning *Harambee* time.

In addition to the social and emotional support they receive Freedom Schools©, scholars report a strong sense of self-esteem and confidence: more than over 80 percent of the children reported having a "good time" and three-quarters felt happy or "like something good is going to happen," despite great loss and trauma. Seventy percent of the children reported they were "just as good as other children," an increase of 13 percent.

This increasing sense of personal pride extends to pride in community and scholars' understanding of their own power. Each summer, Freedom School© staff, scholars, and parents engage in a "Day of Social Action." In 2017, the topic was ending violence and childhood hunger, and Nashville Freedom School students staged demonstrations to raise awareness about the number of children in Nashville and around the world who live with food insecurity and to lend their support to the "Black Lives Matter" movement.

Gordon Freedom School students demonstrate for an end to violence.

Black lives Matter

Stop Slavery

BLACK GIRLS ROCK

In 2018, our theme is voter education and voting rights. Scholars and their teachers are studying the history and impact of the Civil Rights Movement on the involvement of African-Americans and other people of color. They also held their own mock campaigns and elections and encouraged their parents and guardians to register to vote.

Moreover, studies indicate children who attend CDF Freedom Schools© score significantly higher on standardized reading achievement tests than children who attend other summer enrichment programs; African-American middle school boys made the greatest gains of all. Research by our Nashville Freedom Schools' evaluation team find that children and teens who attend Freedom School for two summers or more see an increased the impact on reading achievement.

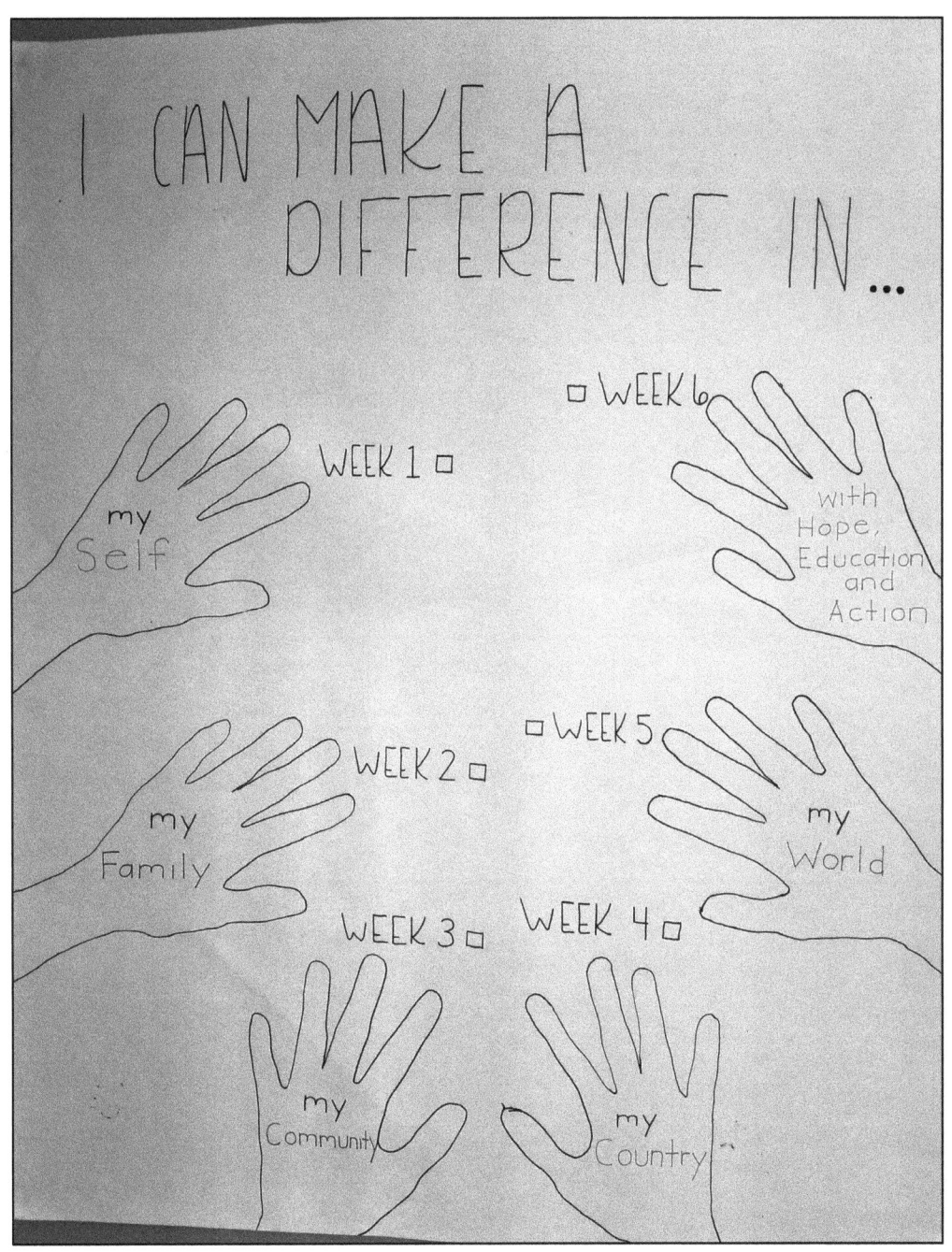

Thanks to our 2018 Evaluation Team: **Dr. Susan Mosley-Howard,** coordinator; **Mary Berlin**; **Kitty Calhoon**; **Janetta Fleming**; **Joseph Gutierrez**; **Christie Bell Harris**; **Sandra Ragin-Haddock**; **Liza Ramage**, and **Dr. Amy Steele**

Gordon scholar, Makenna, who is an excellent reader and singer, has been with Nashville Freedom Schools since our 2014 launch.

DAILY PLAYBOOK

8:00 – 8:30 am	Breakfast
8:30 – 9:00 am	Harambee
9:00 – 10:30 am	Integrated Reading Curriculum 1
10:30 – 10:45 am	Break
10:45 – 11:45 am	Integrated Reading Curriculum 2
11:45 am – 12:00 pm	Drop Everything and Read
12:00 – 1:00 pm	Lunch
1:00 – 3:00 pm	Afternoon Activities
3:00 pm	Dismissal

COOPERATING

Scholars and staff at each site—and in every classroom—create a "cooperation contract" on how we conduct ourselves as individuals and as a Freedom School© community. The concept of 'One Mic,' comes from the hip-hop community, in which rappers share one microphone and, when one person is rapping, others listen respectfully.

SINGING

This is "the crowd singing the Motivational Song while looking at the TV," by Abrielle, age 6 years old.

Something Inside So Strong

Our Motivational Song
(sung every morning at Freedom Schools© across the United States)

The higher you build your barriers
The taller I become
The farther you take my rights away
The faster I will run
You can deny me
You can decide to turn your face away
No matter, cos there's....

Something inside so strong
I know that I can make it
Tho' you're doing me wrong, so wrong
You thought that my pride was gone
Oh no! Something inside so strong
Oh! Something inside so strong

The more you refuse to hear my voice
The louder I will sing
You hide behind walls of Jericho
Your lies will come tumbling
Deny my place in time
You squander wealth that's mine
My light will shine so brightly
It will blind you
Cos there's....

Something inside so strong
I know that I can make it
Tho' you're doing me wrong, so wrong
You thought that my pride was gone
Oh no! Something inside so strong
Oh! Something inside so strong

Brothers and sisters
When they insist we're just not good enough
When we know better
Just look 'em in the eyes and say
I'm gonna do it anyway
I'm gonna do it anyway

Something inside so strong
I know that I can make it
Tho' you're doing me wrong, so wrong
You thought that my pride was gone
Oh no! Something inside so strong
Oh oh oh oh oh something inside so strong

—Written by Labi Siffre, copyright 1984

MEETING

Left:
Local political leaders greet Gordon scholars during a field trip to the Metro Nashville mayor's office.

Below:
Local political leader Howard Gentry greets scholars during a field trip to the Metro Nashville government office.

Gordon Memorial scholar, Aniyah, talks to Kathy FitzJeffries, a social worker from North Carolina who visited with some of our scholars and staff this summer.

ENDJOYING

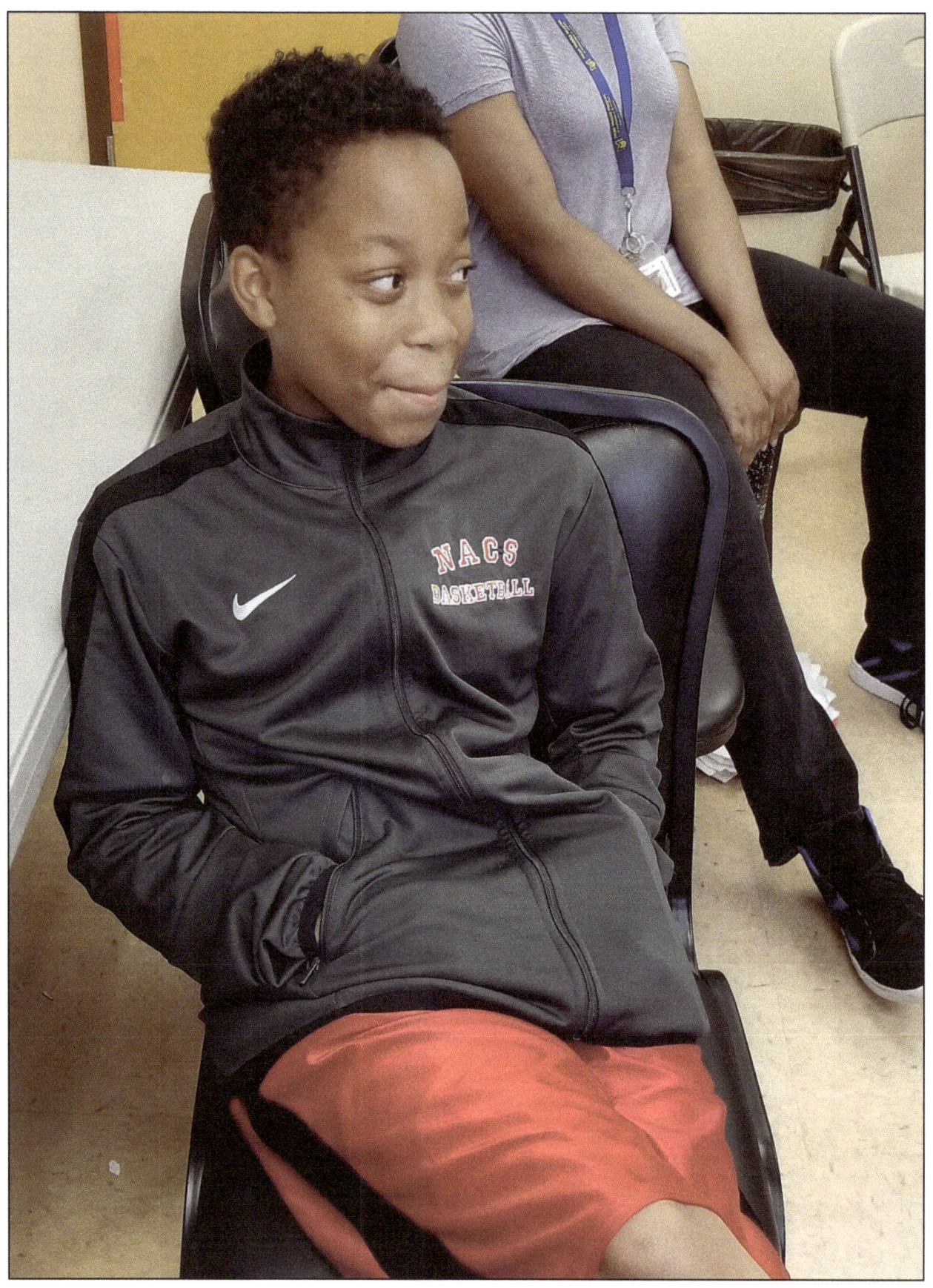

Scholar Donovan enjoys his class discussion.

PERSEVERING

Our Freedom School© goal? To celebrate the greatness of each scholar and encourage them to live it out.

INSPIRING OURSELVES

A scholar's vision board, featuring her heroes and inspirations.

INSPIRING EACH OTHER

The theme of Freedom Schools©' nationally is "I Can Make a Difference," and each week scholars read books about the different ways they can make an impact on home, school, and community. This theme is central to our curriculum and activities.

INSPIRING OTHERS

Above: One of the scholars leads a class lesson.

Right: Gordon Memorial Freedom School student Kamiyah is winning her class' lip-sync battle.

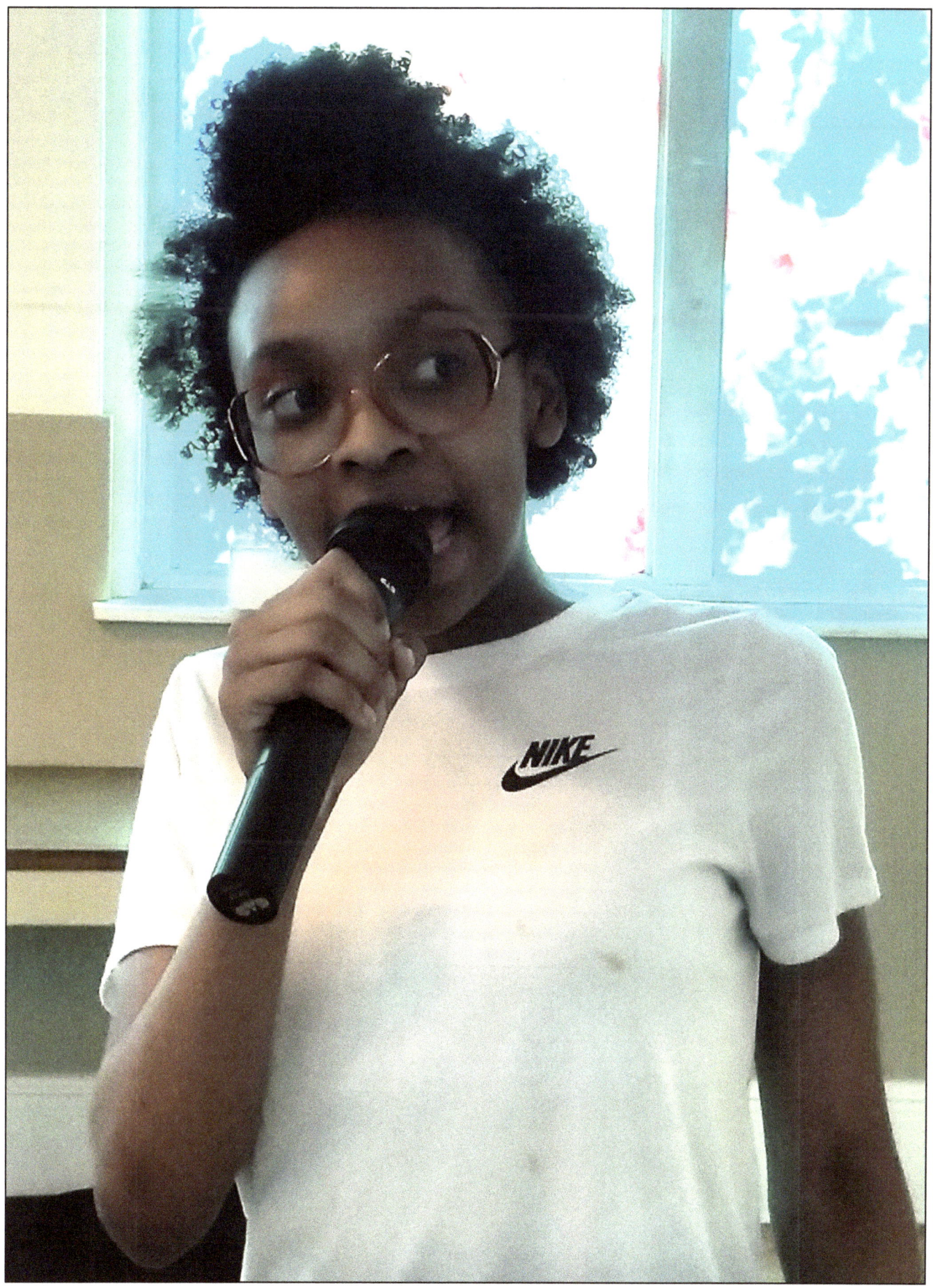

LISTENING

Each morning at Freedom School©, guest readers share a new book or story with our scholars. Here, Phyllis Sells of West End United Methodist Church, reads to children in grades K-4.

Lonnell Matthews, newly elected clerk for Juvenile Court, reads to 2018 Watson Grove scholars.

Cellist Creamaine Booker, left, and Emma Supica of the ALIAS Chamber Ensemble in Nashville entertain Watson Grove scholars.

Above: Lucius "Spoonman" Talley of the National Museum of African American Music in Nashville, beats out rhythms as a guest artist at Watson Grove Freedom School.

Joey Butler, a local journalist and guitarist, wows Gordon Memorial scholars with his skills.

Marcella Tudeen, a Read-Aloud Guest from Brentwood United Methodist Church, reads the book *She Persisted* to scholars at Gordon Memorial's Freedom School. Brentwood members supported Freedom Schools© financially and through volunteer hours this year.

ANALYZING

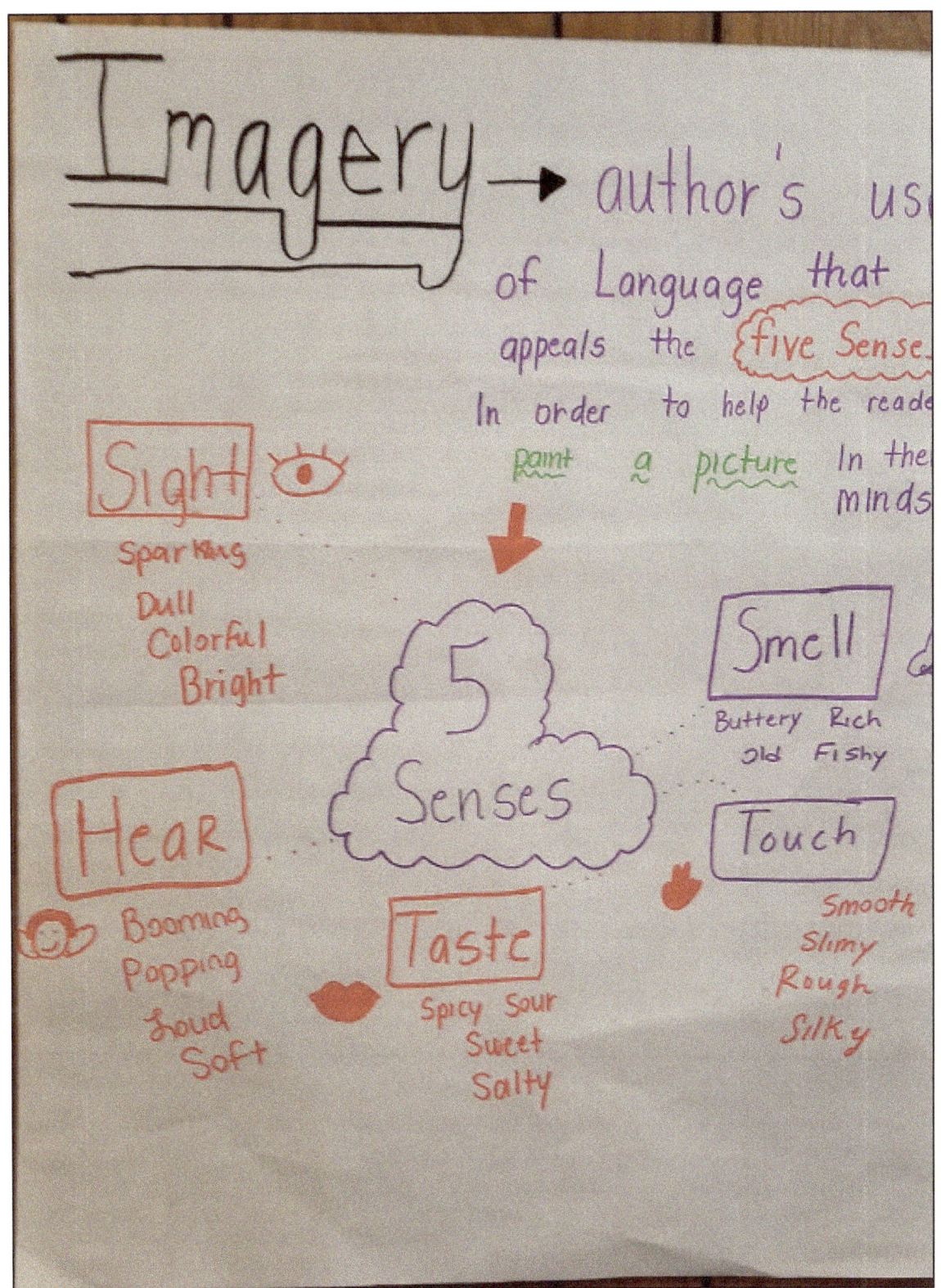

Chart to help scholars analyze and understand the books they read.

READING

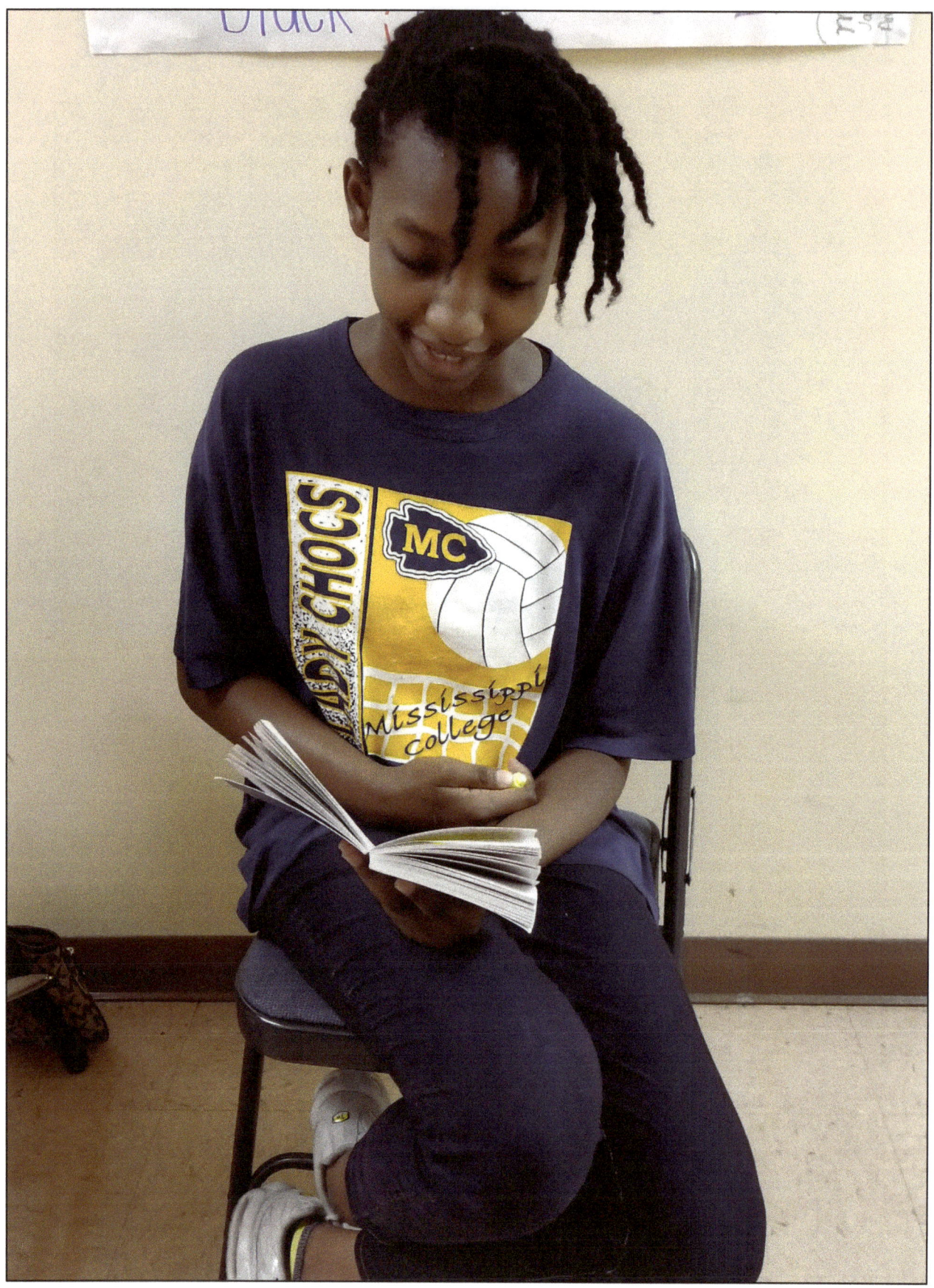

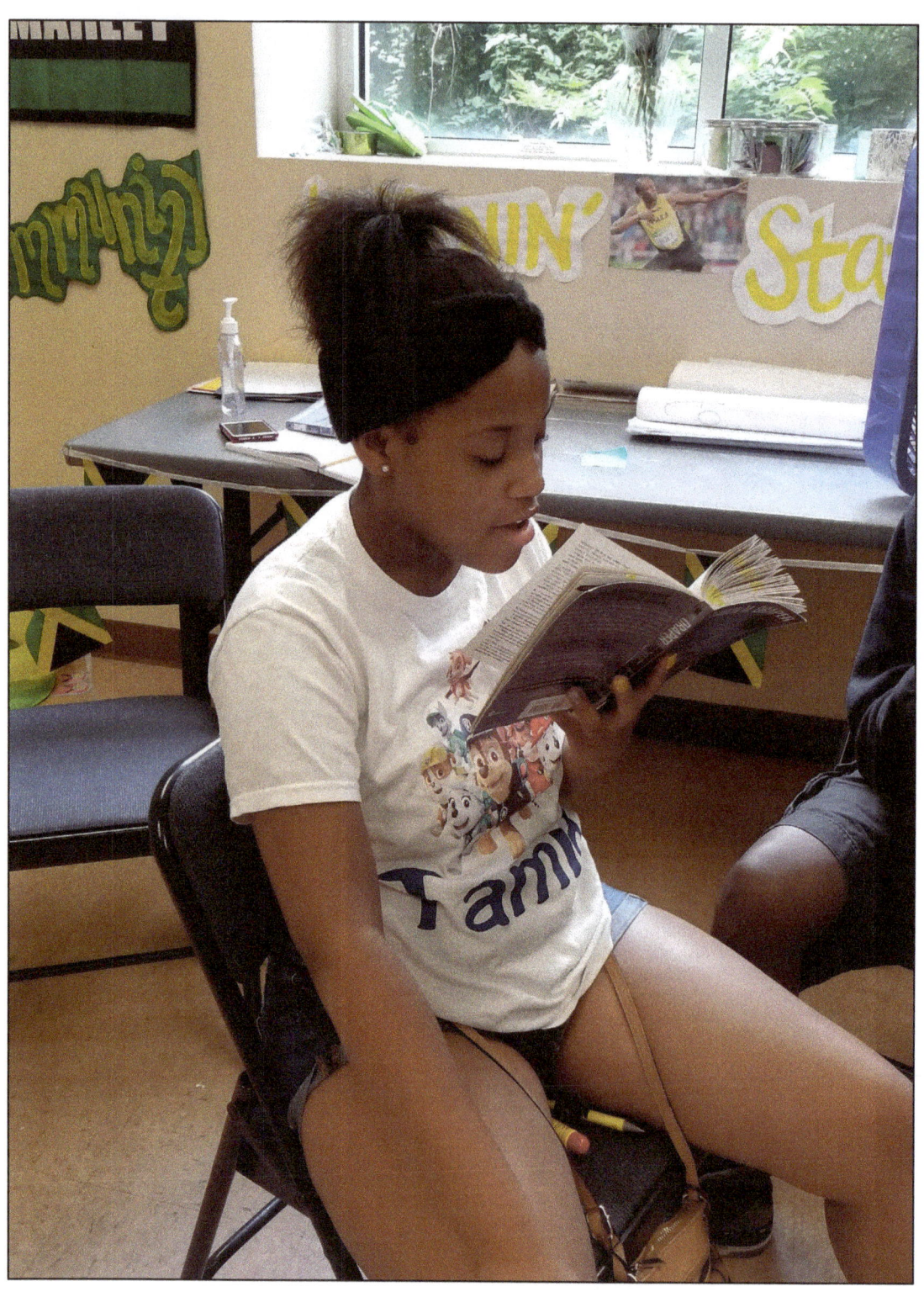

Tamia reads aloud to her classmates.

Emerging as a strong class leader this year, Gordon Memorial scholar Emyjai read to her Freedom School mates.

WRITING

DRAWING

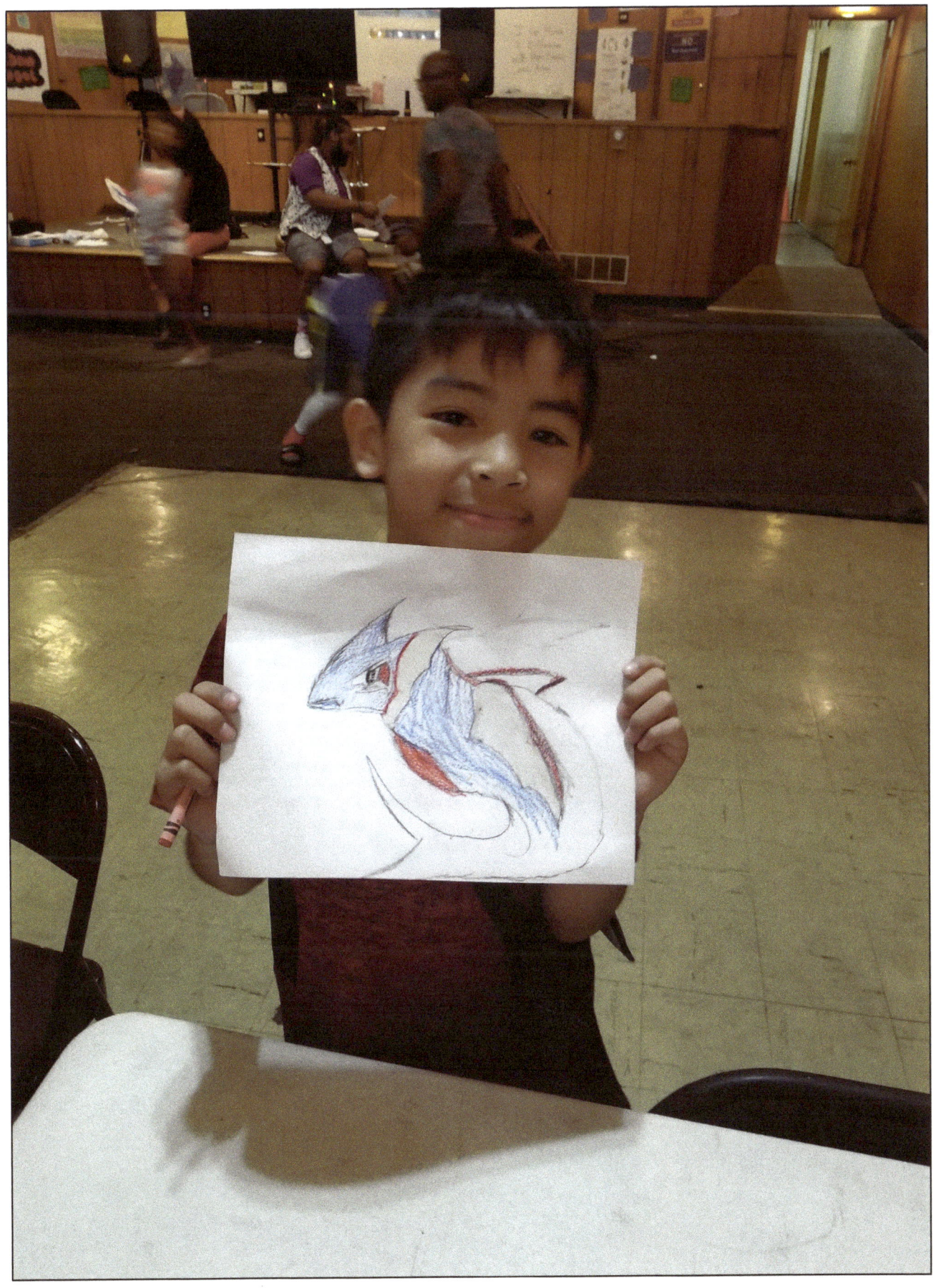

88

COOKING

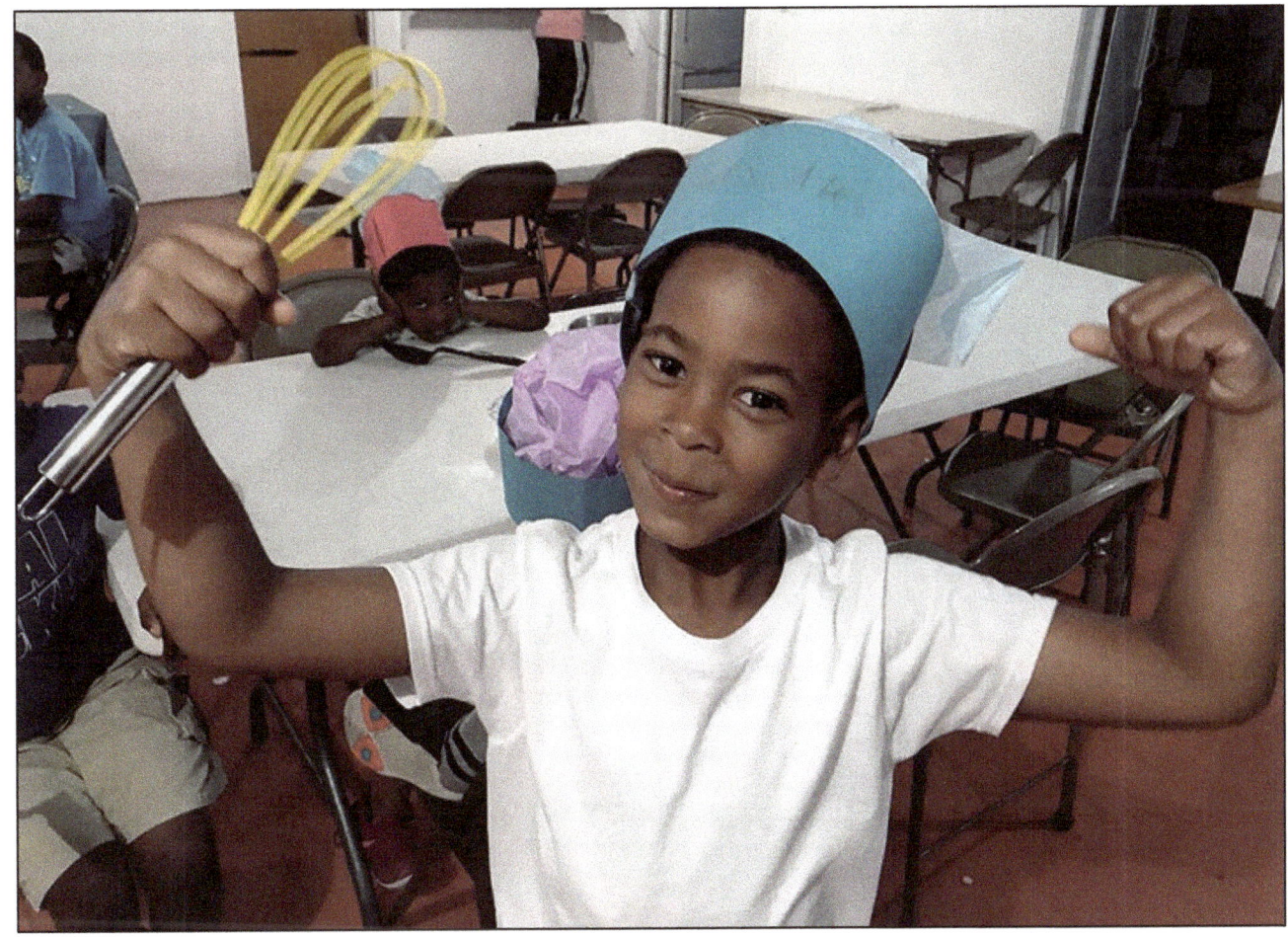

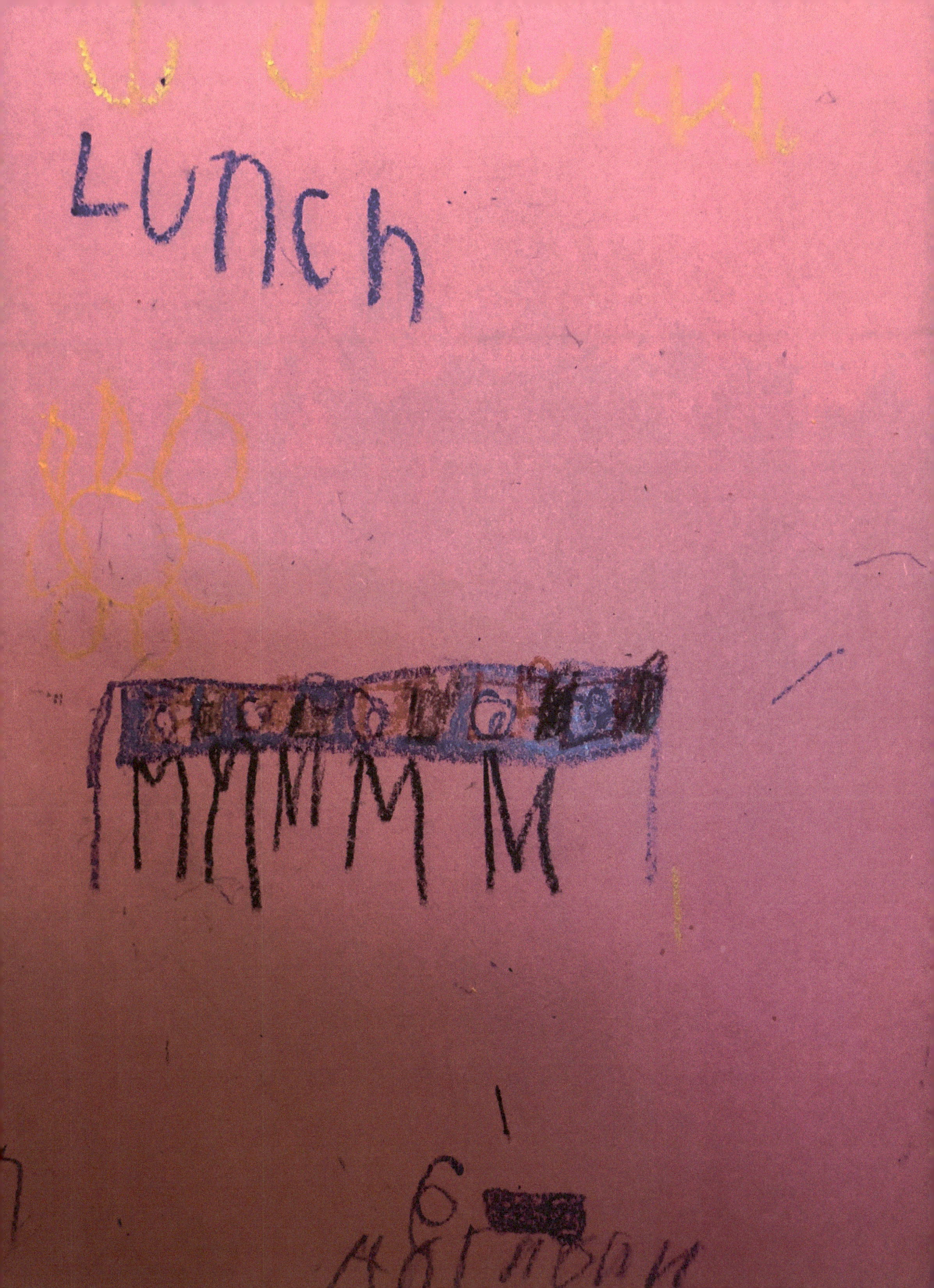

EATING

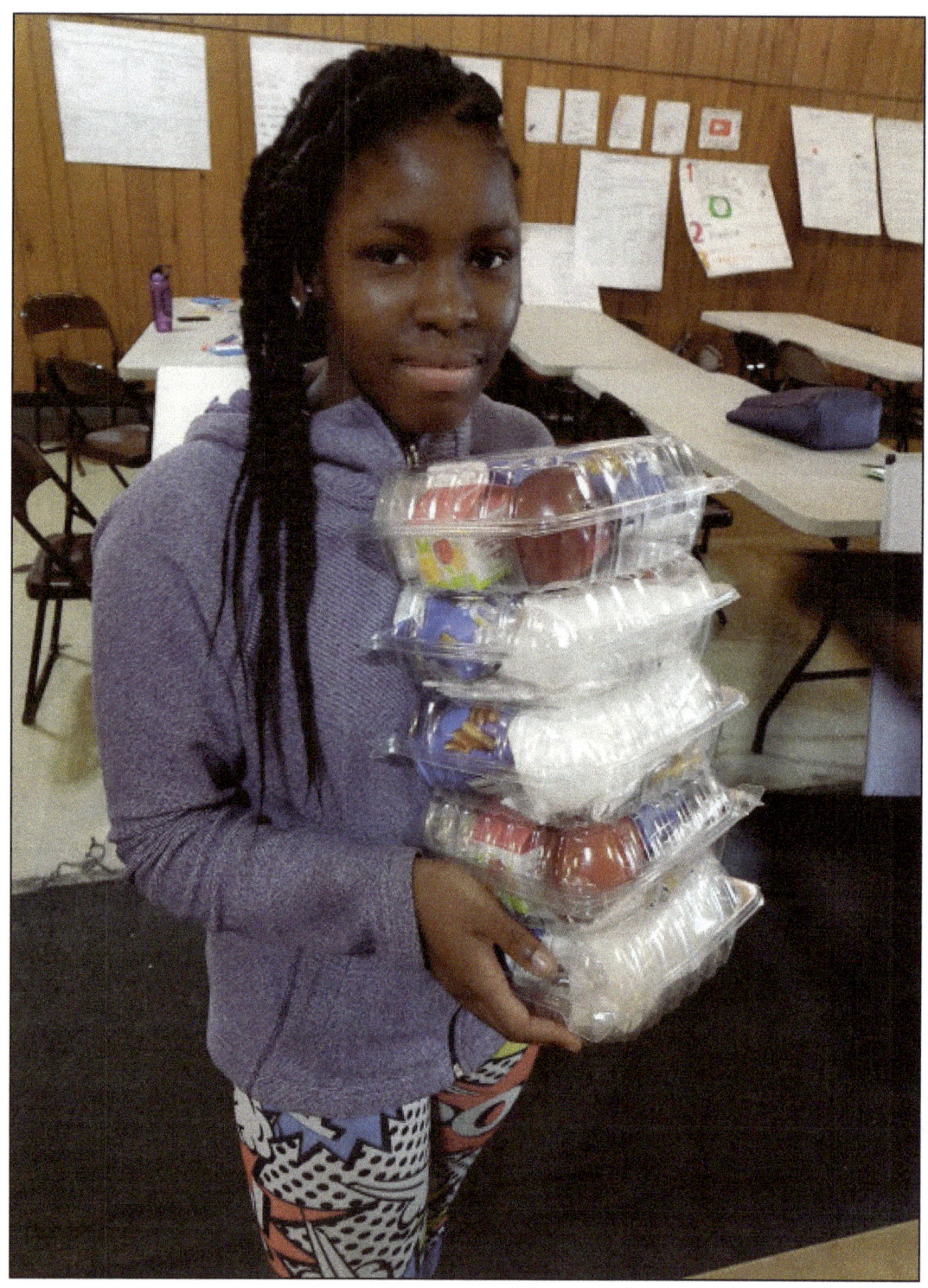

Junior Intern Marquisha Harvey serves lunch at Watson Grove Freedom School.

Thanks to a federal program administered by the Metro Action Commission, breakfast and lunch are provided at no cost to scholars and families. A special thanks to Marvin Cox, who oversees the Commission's summer food program.

2018 intern Chioma Tait enjoys breakfast with her scholars.

Joseph Gutierrez, of the Maddox Foundation of Nashville, shares a smile over breakfast with scholars at our new 2018 Freedom School at Watson Grove Baptist Church. Joseph, a member of the Nashville Freedom School Partnership board of directors, also helped with our scholar evaluations this year.

PARTICIPATING IN SOCIAL ACTIONS

Scholars from the Gordon Memorial Freedom School demonstrate against childhood hunger (above) and in support of voter participation (below) reminding adults, "Your Voice is My Vote." Engaging in positive social action and responsible citizenship are key aspects of our work with scholars and parents.

TESTING

Left: Sandra Ragin-Haddock, a member of sponsor Gordon Memorial United Methodist Church, was one of six volunteers who conducted our pre- and post-test evaluations with our scholars. Dr. Susan Mosely-Howard, a sociologist and professor emeritus of Miami University, designed our testing protocol and trained our evaluators.

Right: Kitty Calhoon, right, a retired educator, encourages a scholar during an evaluation to measure progress in reading and critical thinking.

Left: Christie Bell Harris, an elementary school teacher in Nashville (here with scholar Isaiah), was part of the pre- and post-test evaluations team that helped chart our scholars' progress in reading, critical thinking, and sight-word fluency.

LEARNING

During a field trip to United Methodist Communications, Gordon scholars learn the art of audio production.

2018 scholars learn the history of Judaism in Nashville during a field trip at Temple Ohabai Sholom, a funder and friend of Nashville Freedom Schools.

IMAGINING

Books transport us from the familiar...

to the possible...

to imaginary worlds of mermaids and unicorns and beyond.

CREATING

Clay rendering of a city park, created by a 2018 scholar.

Lauren Tillman (standing), a student at Vanderbilt Divinity School, worked with scholars in developing their own comic books.

Above: Gordon scholars discuss ideas for creating a class comic book.

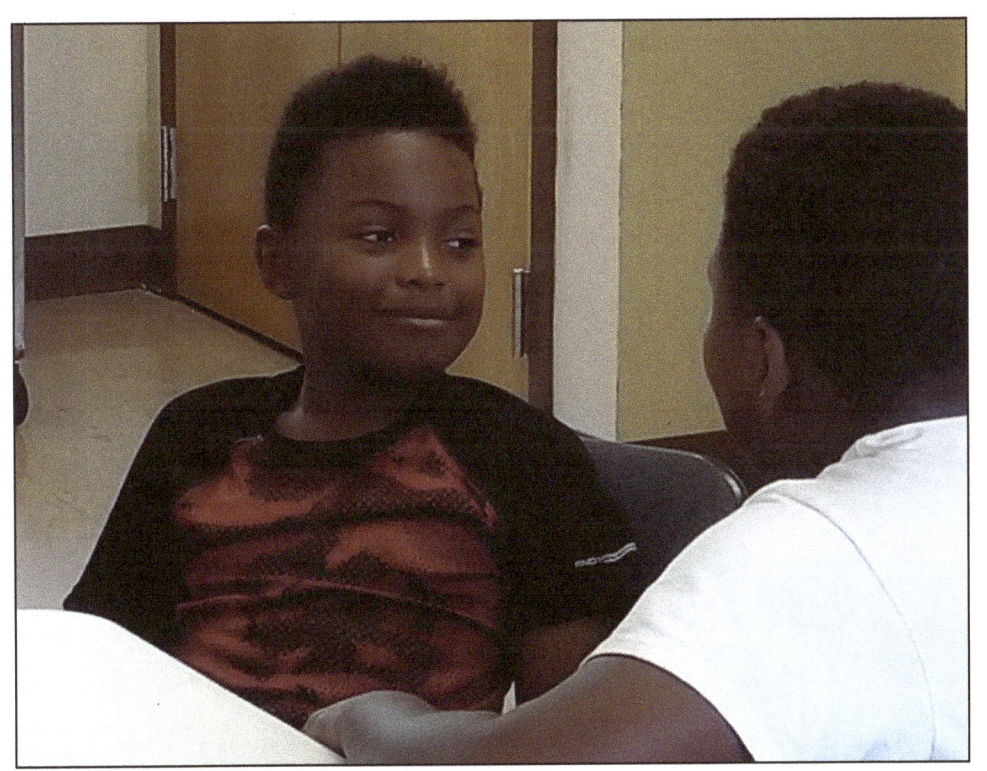

Left:

Gordon scholar Tyriq discuss his favorite comic character, Black Panther.

Watson Grove scholar Jayla models a shirt she decorated in class.

EXPERIENCING

A scholars' first experience picking vegetables during a field trip at the School of Agriculture at Tennessee State University.

RECHARGING

A scholar takes a break from reading classes to express his creative side.

DISCUSSING

Right: Nashville Freedom Schools' board member, Dr. Ernest Patton, a 1964 Freedom Rider, leads a discussion with scholars at the Civil Rights room of the Nashville Public Library.

Below: Members of the class led by 2018 intern Kimberly Morris lead the class discussion on a book about a high school athlete who dies in a car accident.

111

DANCING

Scholars at the 2018 Watson Grove Freedom School learn a new folk dance.

A member of the local folk dance group, Tantsova Grupa,
makes friends with Watson Grove Freedom School student, Josiah.

Members of Tantsova Grupa, a folk dance-and-music group, offered a lesson for children at the 2018 Freedom School at Watson Grove Baptist Church.

DISCOVERING

Above: Field trips expose scholars to new ways of self-expression. Scholars here learn the art of pottery-making.

Below: Goats from the School of Agriculture at Tennessee State University greet Nashville Freedom School scholars during a field trip.

STRETCHING BODIES

Above and below: Volunteer Janetta Fleming teaches yoga at Gordon Memorial's Freedom School.

STRETCHING MINDS

Young men at the Freedom School at Gordon Memorial Church learn strategic thinking by learning chess.

Afternoon math classes.

EMULATING

Left: 2018 Intern Angel Frazier celebrates African heritage day at Gordon Memorial Freedom School.

Below: 2018 intern Terry Blackburn of Fisk University (with a scholar) channels wisdom and mentoring, virtues extolled in the movie "Black Panther," and celebrated at Gordon Memorial Freedom School.

Right: Tiara Clark, intern at Gordon Memorial, dons face paint that mimics African tribal adornment.

Below: Project director MacKenzie Milon, a 2018 graduate of Howard University's master's degree program in social work, applies face paint to a Gordon Memorial scholar during the "Black Panther"-inspired celebration.

EVALUATING

EmmaJulia Jones, a Metro school teacher and graduate of Centre College, keeps her Watson Grove scholars inspired.

Chloe Levin of the national Children's Defense Fund office gave high marks to the new Watson Grove Freedom School during her site visit.

The 2018 Nashville Freedom School Partnership Board of Directors

M. Garlinda Burton, executive director and president
Bill Haley, treasurer
Erica Battle
Dr. Jocelyn D. Briddell
Mike DuBose
Joseph Gutierrez
LaNessa Jackson
Dr. Ernest Patton
Ashiya Swan
Randy Taylor
Wil Taylor
The Rev. Dr. Janet Wolf, at-large

Nashville Freedom School Board Members Janet Wolf (at large) and Bill Haley (treasurer).

Thanks to Our 2018 Financial Supporters

Our 2018 Freedom Riders (financial gifts of $1,000 or more)

Ethel Battle; Brentwood United Methodist Church; Deaconess M. Garlinda Burton; Russell Casteel; Caterpillar Financial Services (via board member LaNessa Jackson); Mike and Jane Gibbs DuBose; Angella Current-Felder; the Fringe Foundation; the General Board of Higher Education and Ministry of the United Methodist Church; Gordon Memorial United Methodist Church; The Rev. Pamela Cunningham Hawkins; Dr. Helen Houston; Andris Salter and Elizabeth McDonald; the Sawyers Family Fund (in honor of board member Ashiya Swan); the Rev. Ray and Phyllis Sells; the Cal Turner Program for Moral Leadership at Vanderbilt University; the Vanderbilt University Office of Community, Neighborhood, and Government Relations; Josefa Bethea Wall; Watson Grove Baptist Church; West End United Methodist Church; the Dale and Clarice Wolf Foundation (the Rev. Dr. Janet Wolf, Glenda Wolf Lingo, Jim Wolf and Tom Wolf); the Rev. Dr. Janet Wolf and Bill Haley.

Our 2018 Ella Baker Donors (financial gifts of $500 to $999)

Rosalyn H. Anderson; Renee and Joey Butler; Danny Epstein; Hohenwald (Tenn.) United Methodist Women; Ronna Case and Ted Jennings; James Melchiorre; Temple Ohabai Sholom.

Our 2018 Nashville Freedom School Boosters (financial gifts of $5 to 499)

Anonymous; Ages & Stages Class of Calvary United Methodist Church in Nashville; Angella Allen; Angie Allen; Linda Bloom and Paul Sommer; Dr. Jocelyn Briddell; Ken Briggs; Christy Brown (in honor of the Rev. Tamila Robertson); Cheryl Capshaw; Raline Center; Pamela Crosby; Sharon Dean; Marie Dunkerson; Gwendolyn L. Felder; the Fellowship of United Methodists in Music and Worship Arts; Kim Goods; April Gung; Joseph Gutierrez; Dr. Phyllis Hildreth; Shantrelle Johnson; Jennifer Joy; Jan Keeling; the Rev. Kathleen LaCamera Loughlin; the Rev. Bettye P. Lewis and Dr. Tamara Lewis; Midori Lockett; Mary Z. and Marcia Longknight; the Rev. Luther Young; Brittany McRay; Biljana Milenkovic; Chris and Mary Sue Moore; Carole E. Nelson (in honor of Liam Charles Cullen's first birthday); the Rev. Kathy Noble; Warren Norman; Betsy Parham; Joanne Reich; Carol B. and John K. Rice; Diane Smith; Joyce Sohl; Dr. Amy Steele; April Stevens; Bishop Melvin and Marilyn Magee Talbert; Tim Tanton and Jama Bowen; D.S. Tibbs and D.M. Malone; Deaconess Liz Shadboldt; Joyce Sohl; Dr. Emilie M. Townes; Dorian Townsend; Stella B. Venson; Janet Walsh; Zona Watkins; Paula C. Watson; Dr. G. Faye Wilson; Woodmont Christian Church; Jamie Woodruff; Sha'Tika Woods; Mary Early Zaid.

Thanks to Our Terrific Community Partners!

The work of the **Nashville Freedom Schools** is made possible because of individual and community partners who donate equipment and snacks, host field trips and special meals, lead fun activities, and give their time as well as resources. It indeed takes a village to nurture our scholars, and the members of our 2018 Freedom School village are:

- ALIAS Chamber Orchestra and Emma Supica, who arranged musical presentations and workshops for our scholars.
- Dr. Jocelyn Briddell, who coordinated our 2018 Read-Aloud guests.
- The Honorable Judge Sheila Calloway and Willie Halliburton of Nashville Juvenile Court, who support and promote Nashville Freedom Schools, and who helped us recruit guest readers.
- Marvin Cox and the Metro Action Commission, who provided meals for our scholars every day.
- The Cal Turner Program for Moral Leadership at Vanderbilt University and graduate students Hannah Allen, Kelsey Davis, and Philip Hathorn, who helped further improve our promotion and evaluation processes.
- The Children's Defense Fund/Nashville Team (and alums), including Eric Brown, Rahim Buford, Ndume Olatushani, and Janet Wolf, who offer constant support.
- The Children's Defense Fund national office in Washington, who makes this life-altering experience possible.
- Pamela Crosby, Heidi Hewitt, Theresa Khur, Scott Spradley, Lucinda Sutton, and Keitha Vincent of the United Methodist Publishing House for donating art supplies and cash to support our 2018 program.
- Angella Current Felder and Linda Fair, of Gordon Memorial, who believed and made others believe it could happen!
- Dr. Susan Douglas, assistant professor at Peabody College, Vanderbilt University, and students Michael Kroeger, KaLea Lehman, and Danielle Maurer, for advising us on pushing our scholar evaluations to the next level.
- Volunteers and Freedom School© grandparent and parent, Beverly Goetzman and Melinda Coston-Skyers, for helping organize our summer 2018 Parent Empowerment events.
- Donna Harrison and Steve Harrison, members of Belmont United Methodist Church, who donated snacks for both sites this summer.
- The Rev. Pamela ("The Paminator") Cunningham Hawkins, who tells our story, donates time and money, and who always shows up and goes the extra mile to support Nashville Freedom Schools.
- Noah Henscheid, who designed our website and keeps it inviting and functional.
- 2017 Intern George Johnson and career placement executive Tashaye B. Woods of Fisk University, who sent us the most staff candidates ever from one university and helped us recruit stellar 2018 Servant Leader Interns.
- "The M&Ms," Marie Dunkerson and Mary Dunn of Gordon Memorial Church, who gave food and encouragement.
- Bishop William McAlilly and the Tennessee Annual Conference of the United Methodist Church, who encouraged our work.
- Cliff Steger of Gordon Memorial UMC, who spoke for all Nashville Freedom Schools and helped get us needed funds.
- Dr. Suzie Taylor, dean of the School of Education, and the staff of Trevecca Nazarene University, for hosting and supporting our local staff training event.
- Tasneem Tewogbola and the Civil Rights Room of the Nashville Public Library, who preserves our history and brings it to life each year for our scholars.

- The Temple Ohabai Sholom for hosting Watson Grove scholars and teaching us about the contributions of Jewish people to Nashville and the world.
- Board member Ashiya Swan for jumping from staff to fundraiser and lead mentor for our Junior Interns. You are a gift!
- Lauren Tillman, Khortlan Becton, and Abbey LaBrecque, all outstanding at , who each sought and are using grants to expand art education at Nashville Freedom Schools this summer.
- The staff of United Methodist Communications, who donated a much-needed LCD projector and who always send many guest readers (and guitarists) our way.
- Dawanna Wade, chief executive officer of Salama Urban Ministries, for hosting our Watson Grove scholars and staff at the performance of *Annie, Jr*. You are talent and graces times ten!
- Keisha Williams, for recruiting Cynthia Anderson (a keeper!), and for leading classroom management, lesson planning, and restorative justice training for our 2018 staff.
- Brenda Wynn, Davidson County Clerk, who helped identify and secure funding sources and kept cheering us on.
- The senior pastors and supportive staff at our host sites, including: the Rev. Charles White Jr., Michelle Malone, and Richard Wilson of Gordon Memorial Church, and the Rev. John R. Faison Jr., children/youth ministries director Nikki Tolliver, and Jasmine Taylor of Watson Grove.

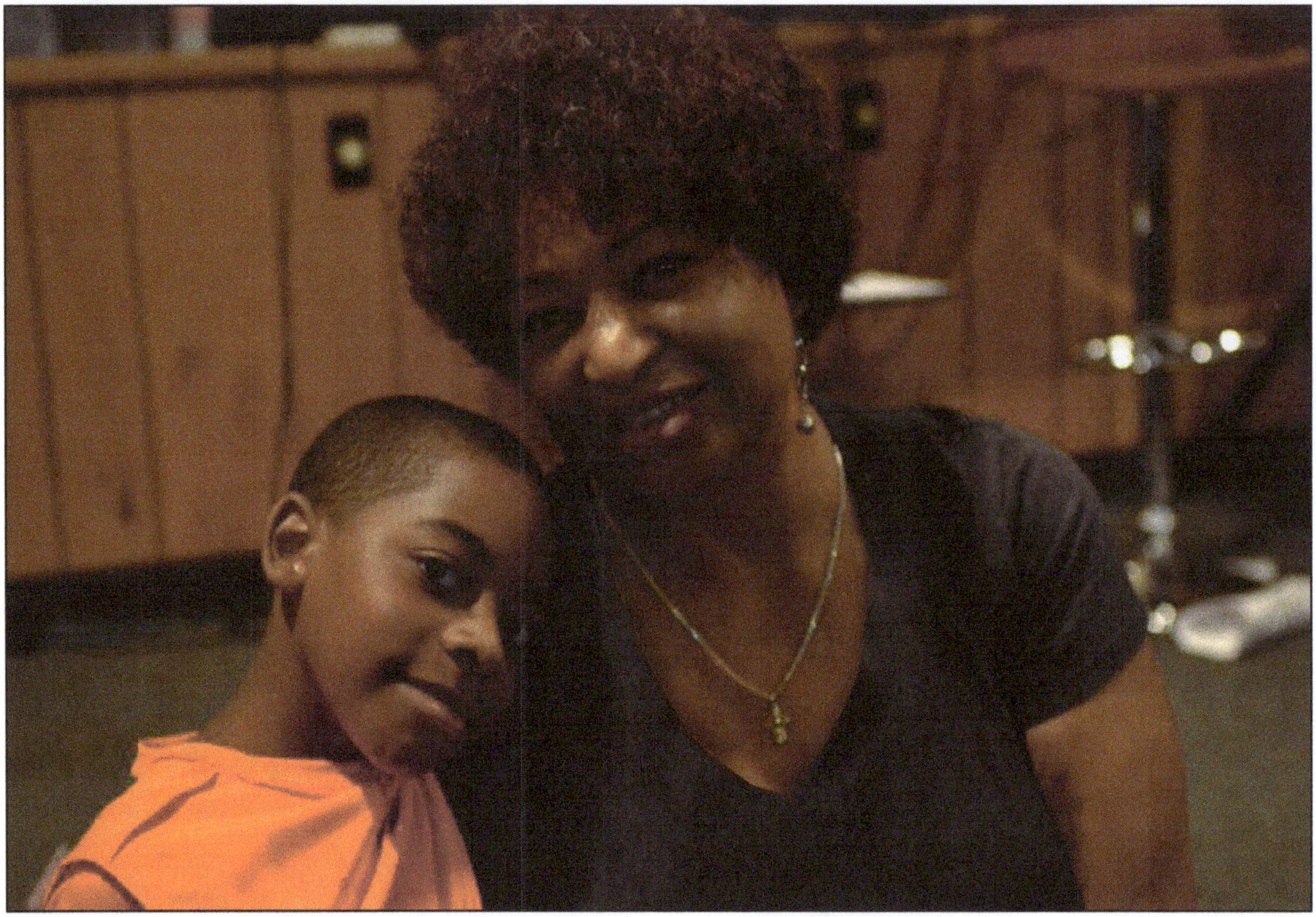

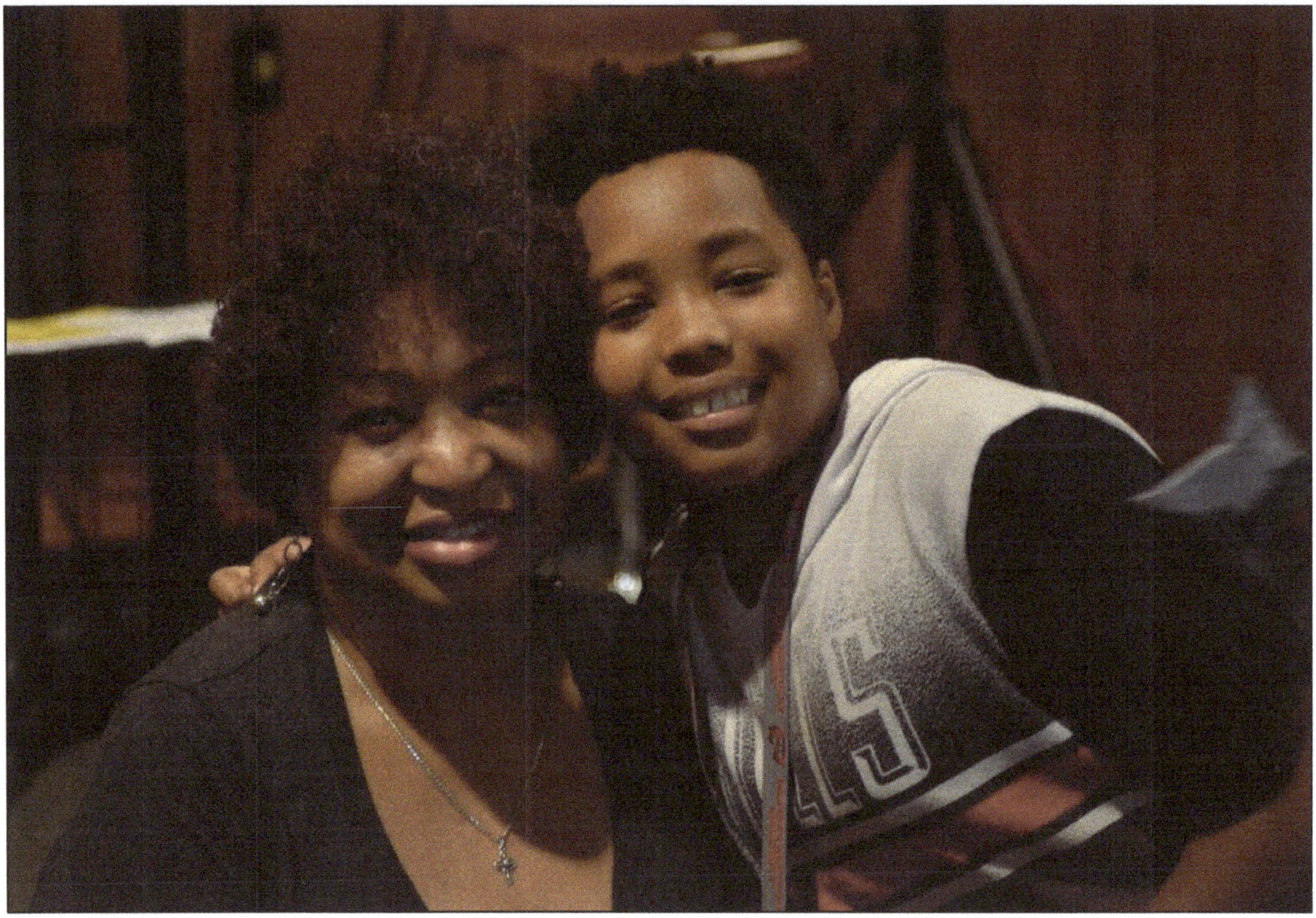

Thanks from our Executive Director

First, many, many thanks to our friend, Mary Catharine Nelson, who published this book and raised funds to provide a copy for every scholar in our 2018 Nashville Freedom Schools; and to authors Bonnie Johnson, Candace Thompson, Carlton Cornett and DeWayne Fulton, George Spain, Ginger Manley, Joyce Carter-Ball, Lorraine Abrams, Sally Lee, and Terry and Barb Gould, for providing those funds. Thanks to the photographers Mike DuBose and Benjamin Johnson for providing wonderful photos. (The bad photos were taken by the director; apologies for my lack of skill.)

Thanks to our scholars and parents for trusting us to become a partner with you in raising up a new, powerful nation of readers and leaders.

Thanks to our financial donors—those who gave much and those who gave more. You make Nashville Freedom Schools possible.

Thanks to the late Ella Baker and the 1964 Freedom Riders and to Marian Wright Edelman and Dr. Janet Wolf of the Children's Defense Fund, for casting a transformational vision.

Thanks for my granddaughter, Sierra Allen-Kizer for sacrificing her summer to do administrative work for me. Bless you, Sweet Pea!

Thanks to my sisters, Newtonia and Jocelyn, for totally having my back.

Thanks to the most energetic Board of Directors that Nashville Freedom Schools have had in a while. Let's keep this party going!

Thanks to our very first Servant Leader Interns, Aneesa, George, Morgan, and Tim, for still supporting everything we do.

Thanks to my mom, Margaret B., for teaching me to love the written word, to every Sunday school and classroom teacher I ever had, and to all the other prayer warriors in my life who encourage this work. You are the wind beneath our wings.

Thanks to the late Clarice Wolf and her family, for believing in us from the beginning.

Rock the Freedom School Forever!

M. Garlinda Burton

Other info:

Nashville Freedom School Partnership is a 501(c)(3) nonprofit registered in the State of Tennessee.

Donate, learn more, and volunteer:

Website: http://nashvillefreedomschools.org
Email: info@nashvillefreedomschools.org

Follow us on Facebook, Twitter, and Instagram
    Nashville Freedom School Partnership
    #NashFreeSchools
    #hollerscholars
    #CDFFreedomSchools
    #RocktheFreedomSchool

Learn more about the Children's Defense Fund Freedom Schools© and other CDF initiatives at http://childrensdefense.org.

Garlinda Burton, the "Grandmother" of Nashville Freedom Schools and author of this book, dances down the purple carpet at Gordon Memorial's *Black Panther*-inspired event.

AUTOGRAPHS

AUTOGRAPHS

AUTOGRAPHS

AUTOGRAPHS

AUTOGRAPHS

AUTOGRAPHS